Renate & Uwe H. Sueltz

GAS STATION

BoD - Books on Demand
Norderstedt - Germany 2019

AF195671

Bibliografische Information durch die Deutsche Nationalbibliothek
Die Deutsche Nationalbibliothek verzeichnet diese Publikation in der
Deutschen Nationalbibliografie; detaillierte bibliografische Daten
sind im Internet über http://dnb.dnb.de abrufbar.

© Renate & Uwe H. Sültz
Herstellung und Verlag:
BoD – Books on Demand, Norderstedt
ISBN 9-78374-1-29760-1

DATE	TOTAL MILES ... DRIVEN	GALLONS	PRICE PER GALLON $	GAS REGULAR PLUS PREMIUM DIESEL	AIR PRESSURE PSI
				drive carefully	

DATE	TOTAL MILES ... DRIVEN	GALLONS	PRICE PER GALLON $	GAS REGULAR PLUS PREMIUM DIESEL	AIR PRESSURE PSI 
				drive carefully	

DATE	TOTAL MILES ... DRIVEN	GALLONS	PRICE PER GALLON $	GAS REGULAR PLUS PREMIUM DIESEL	AIR PRESSURE PSI
				drive carefully	

DATE	TOTAL MILES ... DRIVEN	GALLONS	PRICE PER GALLON	GAS REGULAR PLUS PREMIUM DIESEL	AIR PRESSURE PSI
				drive carefully	

DATE	TOTAL MILES ... DRIVEN	GALLONS	PRICE PER GALLON $	GAS REGULAR PLUS PREMIUM DIESEL	AIR PRESSURE PSI
				drive carefully	

DATE	TOTAL MILES ... DRIVEN	GALLONS	PRICE PER GALLON $	GAS REGULAR PLUS PREMIUM DIESEL	AIR PRESSURE PSI 
				drive carefully	

DATE	TOTAL MILES ... DRIVEN	GALLONS	PRICE PER GALLON $	GAS REGULAR PLUS PREMIUM DIESEL	AIR PRESSURE PSI
				drive carefully	

DATE	TOTAL MILES ... DRIVEN	GALLONS	PRICE PER GALLON	GAS REGULAR PLUS PREMIUM DIESEL	AIR PRESSURE PSI 
				drive carefully	

DATE	TOTAL MILES ... DRIVEN	GALLONS	PRICE PER GALLON $	GAS REGULAR PLUS PREMIUM DIESEL	AIR PRESSURE PSI
				drive carefully	

DATE	TOTAL MILES ... DRIVEN	GALLONS	PRICE PER GALLON	GAS REGULAR PLUS PREMIUM DIESEL	AIR PRESSURE PSI
				drive carefully	

DATE	TOTAL MILES ... DRIVEN	GALLONS	PRICE PER GALLON $	GAS REGULAR PLUS PREMIUM DIESEL	AIR PRESSURE PSI
				drive carefully	

DATE 	TOTAL MILES ... DRIVEN 	GALLONS	PRICE PER GALLON $	GAS REGULAR PLUS PREMIUM DIESEL	AIR PRESSURE PSI 
				drive carefully	

DATE	TOTAL MILES ... DRIVEN	GALLONS	PRICE PER GALLON $	GAS REGULAR PLUS PREMIUM DIESEL	AIR PRESSURE PSI

drive carefully

DATE 	TOTAL MILES ... DRIVEN	GALLONS	PRICE PER GALLON	GAS REGULAR PLUS PREMIUM DIESEL	AIR PRESSURE PSI 
				drive carefully	

DATE	TOTAL MILES ... DRIVEN	GALLONS	PRICE PER GALLON $	GAS REGULAR PLUS PREMIUM DIESEL	AIR PRESSURE PSI
				 **drive carefully**	

DATE	TOTAL MILES ... DRIVEN	GALLONS	PRICE PER GALLON	GAS REGULAR PLUS PREMIUM DIESEL	AIR PRESSURE PSI
				drive carefully	

DATE	TOTAL MILES … DRIVEN	GALLONS	PRICE PER GALLON $	GAS REGULAR PLUS PREMIUM DIESEL	AIR PRESSURE PSI
				drive carefully	

DATE 	TOTAL MILES ... DRIVEN	GALLONS	PRICE PER GALLON $	GAS REGULAR PLUS PREMIUM DIESEL	AIR PRESSURE PSI 
				drive carefully	

DATE	TOTAL MILES ... DRIVEN	GALLONS	PRICE PER GALLON $	GAS REGULAR PLUS PREMIUM DIESEL	AIR PRESSURE PSI
				drive carefully	

DATE 	TOTAL MILES ... DRIVEN	GALLONS	PRICE PER GALLON $	GAS REGULAR PLUS PREMIUM DIESEL	AIR PRESSURE PSI 
				drive carefully	

DATE	TOTAL MILES / ... DRIVEN	GALLONS	PRICE PER GALLON	GAS REGULAR / PLUS / PREMIUM / DIESEL	AIR PRESSURE PSI
				drive carefully	

DATE 	TOTAL MILES ... DRIVEN	GALLONS	PRICE PER GALLON $	GAS REGULAR PLUS PREMIUM DIESEL	AIR PRESSURE PSI 
				drive carefully	

DATE	TOTAL MILES ... DRIVEN	GALLONS	PRICE PER GALLON $	GAS REGULAR PLUS PREMIUM DIESEL	AIR PRESSURE PSI

drive carefully

DATE 	TOTAL MILES ... DRIVEN	GALLONS	PRICE PER GALLON $	GAS REGULAR PLUS PREMIUM DIESEL	AIR PRESSURE PSI 
				drive carefully	

DATE	TOTAL MILES ... DRIVEN	GALLONS	PRICE PER GALLON $	GAS REGULAR PLUS PREMIUM DIESEL	AIR PRESSURE PSI
				drive carefully	

DATE 	TOTAL MILES ... DRIVEN	GALLONS	PRICE PER GALLON $	GAS REGULAR PLUS PREMIUM DIESEL	AIR PRESSURE PSI 
				drive carefully	

drive carefully

DATE	TOTAL MILES ... DRIVEN	GALLONS	PRICE PER GALLON $	GAS REGULAR PLUS PREMIUM DIESEL	AIR PRESSURE PSI

DATE	TOTAL MILES ... DRIVEN	GALLONS	PRICE PER GALLON	GAS REGULAR PLUS PREMIUM DIESEL	AIR PRESSURE PSI
				drive carefully	

DATE	TOTAL MILES ... DRIVEN	GALLONS	PRICE PER GALLON $	GAS REGULAR PLUS PREMIUM DIESEL	AIR PRESSURE PSI
				drive carefully	

DATE 	TOTAL MILES ... DRIVEN	GALLONS	PRICE PER GALLON $	GAS REGULAR PLUS PREMIUM DIESEL	AIR PRESSURE PSI 
				drive carefully	

DATE	TOTAL MILES ... DRIVEN	GALLONS	PRICE PER GALLON $	GAS REGULAR PLUS PREMIUM DIESEL	AIR PRESSURE PSI
				drive carefully	

DATE	TOTAL MILES ... DRIVEN	GALLONS	PRICE PER GALLON	GAS REGULAR PLUS PREMIUM DIESEL	AIR PRESSURE PSI
				drive carefully	

DATE	TOTAL MILES ... DRIVEN	GALLONS	PRICE PER GALLON $	GAS REGULAR PLUS PREMIUM DIESEL	AIR PRESSURE PSI

drive carefully

DATE 	TOTAL MILES ... DRIVEN	GALLONS	PRICE PER GALLON	GAS REGULAR PLUS PREMIUM DIESEL	AIR PRESSURE PSI 
				drive carefully	

DATE	TOTAL MILES ... DRIVEN	GALLONS	PRICE PER GALLON $	GAS REGULAR PLUS PREMIUM DIESEL	AIR PRESSURE PSI
				drive carefully	

DATE	TOTAL MILES ... DRIVEN	GALLONS	PRICE PER GALLON $	GAS REGULAR PLUS PREMIUM DIESEL	AIR PRESSURE PSI
				drive carefully	

DATE	TOTAL MILES / ... DRIVEN	GALLONS	PRICE PER GALLON $	GAS REGULAR PLUS PREMIUM DIESEL	AIR PRESSURE PSI
				drive carefully	

DATE	TOTAL MILES ... DRIVEN	GALLONS	PRICE PER GALLON	GAS REGULAR PLUS PREMIUM DIESEL	AIR PRESSURE PSI

drive carefully

DATE	TOTAL MILES ... DRIVEN	GALLONS	PRICE PER GALLON $	GAS REGULAR PLUS PREMIUM DIESEL	AIR PRESSURE PSI
				drive carefully	

DATE	TOTAL MILES ... DRIVEN	GALLONS	PRICE PER GALLON $	GAS REGULAR PLUS PREMIUM DIESEL	AIR PRESSURE PSI 
				drive carefully	

DATE	TOTAL MILES ... DRIVEN	GALLONS	PRICE PER GALLON $	GAS REGULAR PLUS PREMIUM DIESEL	AIR PRESSURE PSI
				drive carefully	

DATE	TOTAL MILES ... DRIVEN	GALLONS	PRICE PER GALLON	GAS REGULAR PLUS PREMIUM DIESEL	AIR PRESSURE PSI
				drive carefully	

DATE	TOTAL MILES ... DRIVEN	GALLONS	PRICE PER GALLON $	GAS REGULAR PLUS PREMIUM DIESEL	AIR PRESSURE PSI

drive carefully

DATE	TOTAL MILES ... DRIVEN	GALLONS	PRICE PER GALLON $	GAS REGULAR PLUS PREMIUM DIESEL	AIR PRESSURE PSI
				drive carefully	

DATE	TOTAL MILES ... DRIVEN	GALLONS	PRICE PER GALLON $	GAS REGULAR PLUS PREMIUM DIESEL	AIR PRESSURE PSI
				drive carefully	

DATE	TOTAL MILES ... DRIVEN	GALLONS	PRICE PER GALLON	GAS REGULAR PLUS PREMIUM DIESEL	AIR PRESSURE PSI
				drive carefully	

DATE 	TOTAL MILES ... DRIVEN	GALLONS	PRICE PER GALLON $	GAS REGULAR PLUS PREMIUM DIESEL	AIR PRESSURE PSI 
				drive carefully	

DATE	TOTAL MILES ... DRIVEN	GALLONS	PRICE PER GALLON $	GAS REGULAR PLUS PREMIUM DIESEL	AIR PRESSURE PSI
				drive carefully	

DATE	TOTAL MILES / ... DRIVEN	GALLONS	PRICE PER GALLON $	GAS REGULAR PLUS PREMIUM DIESEL	AIR PRESSURE PSI
				drive carefully	

DATE 	TOTAL MILES ... DRIVEN	GALLONS	PRICE PER GALLON $	GAS REGULAR PLUS PREMIUM DIESEL	AIR PRESSURE PSI 
				drive carefully	